ARTIFICIAL INTELLIGENCE
Promise and Peril

John Allen

San Diego, CA

About the Author
John Allen is a writer who lives in Oklahoma City.

© 2024 ReferencePoint Press, Inc.
Printed in the United States

For more information, contact:
ReferencePoint Press, Inc.
PO Box 27779
San Diego, CA 92198
www.ReferencePointPress.com

ALL RIGHTS RESERVED.
No part of this work covered by the copyright hereon may be reproduced or used in any form or by any means—graphic, electronic, or mechanical, including photocopying, recording, taping, web distribution, or information storage retrieval systems—without the written permission of the publisher.

Picture Credits:
Cover: Andrey Suslov/Shutterstock

4: EQRoy/Shutterstock; Hethers/Shutterstock
5: roibu/Shutterstock; JCDH/Shutterstock
8: Maury Aaseng
11: Valerio Rosati/Alamy Stock Photo
12: World History Archive/Alamy Stock Photo
17: Ezio Petersen/UPI Photo Service/Newscom
22: Andresr/iStock
25: Juan Ci/Shutterstock

27: Gorodenkoff/Shutterstock
31: Aleksandr Lupin/Shutterstock
34: Ascannio/Shutterstock
37: Dem10/iStock
41: APChael/Shutterstock
43: Sviatoslav_Shevchenko/Shutterstock
47: Abaca Press/SalamPix/Abaca/Sipa USA/Newscom
50: Abaca Press/Alamy Stock Photo
55: Jason Richardson/Alamy Stock Photo

LIBRARY OF CONGRESS CATALOGING-IN-PUBLICATION DATA

Names: Allen, John, 1957- author.
Title: Artificial Intelligence: Promise and Peril / by John Allen
Description: San Diego, CA : ReferencePoint Press, Inc., 2024.
| Includes bibliographical references and index.
Identifiers: LCCN 2023038802 (print) | ISBN
 9781678207243 (library binding) | ISBN 9781678207250 (ebook)
Subjects: LCSH: Artificial intelligence--Social aspects--Juvenile
 literature. Technological innovations--Juvenile literature.

CONTENTS

Important Events in the History of Artificial Intelligence   **4**

Introduction   **6**
A Question for ChatGPT

Chapter One   **10**
Teaching Machines to Think

Chapter Two   **20**
AI and Smart Homes

Chapter Three   **30**
Medical Uses for AI

Chapter Four   **39**
AI and the Military

Chapter Five   **48**
The AI Revolution in Business

Source Notes   57
For Further Research   60
Index   62

Important Events in the History of Artificial Intelligence

1955
American computer scientist John McCarthy coins the term *artificial intelligence* at a summer AI conference at Dartmouth College.

1960
J.C.R. Licklider of the Massachusetts Institute of Technology (MIT) proposes a fusion of humans and machines in his paper "Man-Computer Symbiosis."

1950
Britain's Alan Turing devises the Turing test to measure the level of machine intelligence.

1968
Stanley Kubrick's film *2001: A Space Odyssey* features a rogue AI computer that kills all but one member of a spaceship crew.

1930　　1950　　1970　　1990

1941
British mathematicians use the principles of AI to break the Germans' Enigma military code.

1973
Great Britain's Lighthill report raises questions about AI research and leads to an end of government support for the technology.

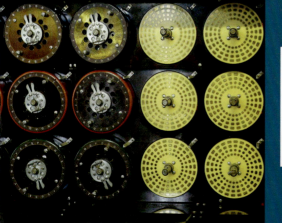

1964
MIT professor Joseph Weizenbaum creates ELIZA, the first chatbot.

1993
Mathematician Vernor Vinge predicts that machines will surpass humans in intelligence in thirty years—the so-called singularity.

2000
MIT's Cynthia Breazeal publishes her research on sociable machines and Kismet, a robot with a face that can express emotions.

2004
The National Aeronautics and Space Administration's robotic rovers navigate the surface of Mars autonomously.

2009
Google uses AI to create Project Chauffeur for self-driving cars.

2015
Tech experts and scientists, including Stephen Hawking and Elon Musk, sign an open letter to ban development and use of autonomous weapons.

2000 — 2010 — 2020 — 2030

2011
Apple launches its voice-activated virtual assistant Siri for the iPhone.

2023
At a White House meeting, seven of the top AI companies in the United States agree to voluntary safeguards on the technology's development.

2002
The company iRobot introduces Roomba, an efficient AI-powered vacuum cleaner.

2020
OpenAI introduces GPT-3, a chatbot that can generate text from a prompt.

INTRODUCTION

A Question for ChatGPT

In April 2023 the computer app ChatGPT was all the rage in news reports and on social media. The app is based on artificial intelligence, or AI, that enables a computer program to tap vast amounts of online information and generate coherent textual responses to user questions or prompts. Intrigued, a South Dakota blogger named Tony Venhuizen asked the program to write a blog post that discussed South Dakota's oldest and youngest governors. In less than a minute, ChatGPT responded with a very respectable-looking essay. The prose was clear, the paragraphs well organized. There was a problem though. Most of the facts were wrong, including names and dates. Worst of all, the AI-powered app had at one point created a South Dakota governor out of thin air. It even provided a portrait of the phony official. Venhuizen reacted to the app's fabrications with a mixture of amusement and mild alarm. "Most notably, Crawford H. 'Chet' Taylor was never governor of South Dakota," he says, "and, in fact, I can find no evidence of such a person, at all. I will credit ChatGPT, though, that Governor Taylor is a plausible-sounding fictional governor."[1]

Debate over AI's Impact

The appearance of ChatGPT brought a new focus to the debate over AI and how it might affect the future. Curious users rushed to download the app and try it out for themselves. They asked it all sorts of questions, some serious (How can we solve the problem of homelessness?) and some not so serious (How do you plan to take over the world?). Politicians saw it as a valuable source for policy and speech ideas, while students dreamed of all the book reports it could write. Users marveled at the vast amount of information it was able to access. And like Venhuizen, some found that the app was prone to making things up, or hallucinating, as tech experts called it. Most agreed, however, that even ChatGPT's flaws were fascinating. And random fabrications aside, ChatGPT typically produced quite serviceable prose, and the technology was improving rapidly.

Excitement over AI's prospects bubbled up overnight. Stock analysts tabbed it as the next game-changing technology, akin to the internet, personal computer, and smartphone. Companies with AI expertise saw their stock prices shoot higher. A 2023 World Economic Forum report estimated that AI would create 97 million new jobs. Other forecasts saw it boosting the global economy by trillions of dollars. According to AI advocates, its ability to gather and sift information at incredible speed will enable workers to become more efficient and productive overall. They predict that apps like ChatGPT will soon become valued assistants in hospitals, medical clinics, law offices, science labs, military bases, and anywhere else that rapid data analysis is key. And one day AI-powered robots could take over as twenty-four-hour caregivers for the disabled or elderly, without becoming tired or bored.

> **"AI won't take your job. It's somebody using AI that will take your job."[2]**
>
> —Richard Baldwin, economist at the Geneva Graduate Institute

Nonetheless, there was no shortage of opposing views. Some economists warned that it could be more of a job killer than job creator. The World Economic Forum report also found that more than 80 million jobs could be lost to AI. Translators and paralegals (law office assistants who organize files and do legal research) are among those who might suddenly find themselves replaced by a computer app. As a result, whole industries could be upended. Analysts warn that workers need to learn the new technology to protect themselves. "AI won't take your job," says Richard Baldwin, an economist at the Geneva Graduate Institute in Switzerland. "It's somebody using AI that will take your job."[2]

Americans Feel More Concern than Excitement When It Comes to AI

Growing use of artificial intelligence (AI) in daily life leaves Americans feeling more concerned than excited, according to a Pew Research Center poll published in February 2023. Among US adults overall, only 15 percent say they are more excited than concerned. Even when grouped by level of awareness of AI's role in daily life, the outcome is essentially the same. Regardless of whether they have a high, medium, or low level of awareness, the percentage who feel excitement is lower than the percentage who feel concern.

Percentage of US adults who say the increased use of artificial intelligence in daily life makes them feel . . .

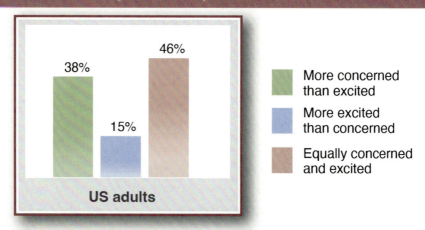

Among those who have a _____ level of awareness of artificial intelligence applications in daily life

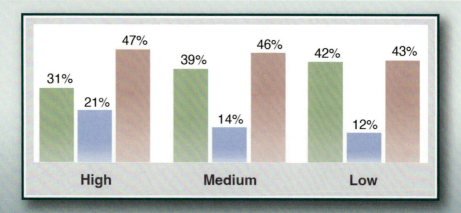

Note: Respondents who did not give an answer are not shown.
Source: Brian Kennedy et al, "Public Awareness of Artificial Intelligence in Everyday Activities," February 15, 2003. www.pewresearch.org.

Another worry is that ChatGPT and other AI apps will spread misinformation. Venhuizen's fake South Dakota governor is just one example of how unreliable AI's output can be. Experts fear that people could turn to ChatGPT for medical advice or for help in making crucial life decisions. As Arizona State University computer science professor Subbarao Kambhampati notes, "There is no guarantee that these systems will be correct on any task you give them."[3] Moreover, as ChatGPT learns to communicate like another person, users may find its conclusions persuasive to a dangerous degree.

An Evolving Technology

Both sides of the debate agree that ChatGPT and other AI apps are still in their early stages and still evolving. ChatGPT itself—which was developed by OpenAI, a San Francisco–based company—is not a brand-new technology. In fact, the latest version that has caused such a furor is ChatGPT-4. Like its predecessors, it is a neural network, or math system, that can learn to do things by analyzing vast amounts of data. This data, made up of digital text on the internet, forms so-called large language models, or LLMs. One of ChatGPT-4's key improvements is its ability to incorporate visual data from text descriptions. AI scientists hope to one day incorporate machine learning directly from visual images and sounds, closer to how the human brain processes data.

AI's rapid evolution also raises questions about whether it could someday develop beyond its creators' control. In such a case, experts warn, it could endanger all of humanity. In March 2023 an open letter signed by more than one thousand tech leaders and scientists warned that AI technology was becoming a threat to society and even risked extinction of humanity. The signers urged the AI industry to pause for at least six months to examine the risks. Such a pause for a global industry remains unlikely, but the concerns about AI continue to grow. "Our ability to understand what could go wrong with very powerful A.I. systems is very weak," admits Yoshua Bengio, an AI researcher at the University of Montreal who also signed the open letter, "so we need to be very careful."[4]

CHAPTER ONE

Teaching Machines to Think

For the head of a tech company, it makes the ideal employee: a new programmer that can write code in twenty computer languages, including JavaScript, TypeScript, and Python. And when asked a question about coding, it produces the answer at once, phrased clearly and logically and neatly spaced for easy reading, with hyperlinks to pertinent examples. Plus, this programmer can gather and search through terabytes of information from databases around the world, in English or any of forty other languages. Who wouldn't hire such a remarkable talent!

The name of this programmer is Bard. Like ChatGPT and other AI-powered chatbots, this Google experiment uses AI to generate text, images, and other media from prompts. On May 10, 2023, Sissie Hsiao, vice president and general manager of Google, delivered updates on Bard to a gathering of tech experts and Google employees at the Shoreline Amphitheater in Mountain View, California. As she demonstrated Bard's ability to streamline the coding process and troubleshoot problems on the fly, the programmers in the crowd erupted into cheers and applause. They could see how the updates would make their jobs easier. Hsiao also showed off Bard's facility in helping with everyday tasks. In seconds it used simple prompts to create an invitation for her seven-year-old daughter's birthday party, complete with a unicorn and cake with candles. "When we combine human imagination with Bard's generative AI capabilities, the possibilities are boundless," Hsiao told the audience. "We can't wait to see what you create with it."[5]

> "When we combine human imagination with Bard's generative AI capabilities, the possibilities are boundless. We can't wait to see what you create with it."[5]
>
> —Sissie Hsiao, vice president and general manager of Google

Turing and the Beginnings of AI

The wonders performed by AI apps like Bard and ChatGPT have more than fulfilled the hopes of the early pioneers in artificial intelligence. They would doubtless be impressed by AI's current capabilities—but probably not all that surprised. Predictions about AI's possibilities go back decades. Ironically, one of the technology's earliest breakthroughs came before the concept even had a name.

In the late 1930s Adolf Hitler's German armies threatened to overrun Europe and invade Great Britain. In September 1939 a small group of British math experts set out to crack the Enigma code, a letter-for-letter substitution code the German military used to encrypt its messages. The British mathematician Alan

Google's AI-powered chatbot, Bard, can write code in twenty computer languages, search through terabytes of information from databases around the world, and when asked questions, it can provide clear, logical answers.

Turing built a computing device he called the Bombe, based on the work of code breakers in Poland. It comprised a series of 108 drums, each containing all 26 letters on its face. The drums would rotate electrically to test each possible letter substitution in the thousands of possible combinations. Since the code changed daily, the team also employed educated guesses about what the German messages were likely to contain. For example, the team reasoned that nearly every message would include the phrase *Heil Hitler*—an insight that gave the code breakers letter combinations that they could anticipate and use to unscramble the rest of the code more quickly. It took them six months to make their first breakthrough, and they continued to refine their approach till the war's end. Military experts reckon that the efforts of Turing and his team shortened World War II by at least two years and saved millions of lives.

The Bombe, an electro-mechanical device used by British cryptologists to decipher encrypted messages of the Germans during World War II, is considered to be a predecessor of today's AI technology. A reconstructed device is shown here.

After the war Turing continued to explore the potential for what he called intelligent machinery. He envisioned a computer that could perform multiple functions through a program stored in its memory. He created a chess-playing computer, the Turochamp. In 1950 he came up with what he considered a crucial test for AI systems in the future. The test would discover whether a computer could carry on a conversation that was so humanlike it was impossible to tell it was a machine. The test, called the imitation game or Turing test, became a widely recognized benchmark for artificial intelligence.

The Turing team's role in breaking the Enigma code remained so secret that it was not made public until the 1970s. It took another twenty years for the full story to be revealed. In a 2017 experiment, a state-of-the-art AI app was able to crack the Enigma code in just thirteen minutes using vast amounts of data about the German language. It was proof that Turing's insights into machine intelligence had borne amazing fruit. According to Gavin Brown, professor of machine learning at the University of Manchester, "[Turing's] legacy can be seen right across the University, with researchers developing super computers that can model the human brain, exploring number theory and cryptography, as well as training robots to understand language. Right here, people are working on the principles that he laid down and the dreams that he had."[6]

Carrying on the Quest for AI

Turing died in June 1954, just days short of his forty-second birthday. However, a summer workshop held the following year on the Hanover, New Hampshire, campus of Dartmouth College served to carry on his research in computer science. John McCarthy, a math professor at Dartmouth, organized the meeting along with Marvin Minsky, Nathaniel Rochester, and Claude Shannon. In his 1955 proposal for the workshop, McCarthy coined the term *artificial intelligence* and laid out the basis of the group's work: "We propose that a 2 month, 10 man study of artificial intelligence be

13

> "The study is to proceed on the basis . . . that every aspect of learning or any other feature of intelligence can in principle be so precisely described that a machine can be made to simulate it."[7]
>
> —John McCarthy, math professor at Dartmouth College

carried out during the summer of 1956 at Dartmouth College. . . . The study is to proceed on the basis of the conjecture that every aspect of learning or any other feature of intelligence can in principle be so precisely described that a machine can be made to simulate it."[7]

Science historians consider the Dartmouth workshop to be the founding event in AI research. It brought together experts in mathematics, computer science, and cognitive psychology. Topics in the workshop ranged widely, from problem solving and language processing to neural networks and creativity. The group discussed the neural network as a blueprint for teaching computers to process data through interconnected nodes, much like a human brain. They explored ways of writing rules to program a computer to use language. They debated whether machines could be taught to think independently or merely to imitate human thought. Most important, three workshop participants unveiled a computer program they had designed called the Logic Theorist. Funded by the RAND Corporation, the program mimicked human problem-solving skills and could create proofs that were superior to the work of human mathematicians. Many consider the Logic Theorist to be the first true AI program. Overall, the Dartmouth workshop set the parameters for AI research for years to come.

AI Winter and Dystopian Views

The 1950s saw a rush of excitement about the possibilities for artificial intelligence, culminating in 1959 with a paper by computer scientist Arthur Samuel. In "Some Studies in Machine Learning Using the Game of Checkers," Samuel described how a computer could use examples to learn and draw inferences from patterns in data. In 1960 J.C.R. Licklider of the Massachusetts Institute of Technology proposed a sort of fusion of humans and machines. Licklider announced, "The hope is that, in not too many years, human brains and computing machines will be coupled together very tightly, and that the resulting partnership will think as no human brain has ever thought."[8]

For many scientists and nonscientists alike, such a human-computer symbiosis sounded more like Frankenstein's monster than a recipe for progress. Literature and movies began to take a more skeptical view of AI. In Herbert Goldstone's 1953 short story "Virtuoso," a robot plays a Beethoven sonata on the piano so beautifully that it brings its maestro owner to tears. But the robot refuses to share its playing with the world. "Music is not for robots. It is for man," he tells the maestro. "To me it is easy, yes. . . . It was not meant to be easy."[9]

Some films depicted AI-powered computers as potential killers. In Stanley Kubrick's 1968 movie *2001: A Space Odyssey*, a spacecraft's onboard computer named HAL murders all but one of the crew members. The surviving astronaut must disable HAL in order to save his own life. In *The Terminator* (1984), a cyborg assassin travels back in time to kill a woman whose future son will one day lead an uprising against a world-dominating AI system.

Passing the Turing Test

From time to time, science reporters and tech blogs relay the news that a computer has passed the Turing test. This is the famous test devised by Alan Turing to see whether a computer could successfully fool a questioner into thinking it is human. In 2014 a professor of cybernetics at the University of Reading in Great Britain caused a stir with his claim to have passed the test with a supercomputer program he called Eugene Goostman. Skeptical scientists denied the breakthrough, noting that "Goostman," with a software persona that mimicked a wisecracking Ukrainian thirteen-year-old, was carefully crafted to fool the judges and pass the test.

In June 2022 a Google engineer named Blake Lemoine proclaimed his own Turing triumph with a large language model–equipped chatbot called LaMDA. Lemoine insisted that the tests showed LaMDA to be not merely intelligent but also conscious and self-aware. However, scientists also dismissed Lemoine's claims. "I don't think it's an advance toward intelligence," says Gary Marcus, a cognitive scientist and author. "It's an advance toward fooling people that you have intelligence." Meanwhile, Mustafa Suleyman, cofounder of DeepMind, suggested an updated Turing test for the modern world: give a computer $100,000 and see if it can turn it into $1 million.

Quoted in Will Oremus, "Google's AI Passed a Famous Test—and Showed How the Test Is Broken," *Washington Post*, June 17, 2022. www.washingtonpost.com.

These bleak visions of AI arose during periods of so-called AI winter, when investment in the technology was faltering and computers still lacked the processing power to mimic intelligence. Suggestions that AI-powered machines might replace humanity continued to alarm the faint of heart, while the inability of new computers to pass the Turing test discouraged the most tech-savvy investors. Aside from a brief revival of interest in the early 1980s, AI research withdrew into a niche area for specialists.

Moore's Law and the Resurgence of AI

Focus on AI came roaring back in the 1990s. In 1993, mathematician and science-fiction author Vernor Vinge predicted that within thirty years machines would surpass humans in intelligence. Vinge called this the technological singularity. Rapid advances in AI were due in large part to Moore's law and its effect on computing power. Moore's law is an observation by Gordon Moore, a computer expert and founder of tech giant Intel. Moore noted in 1965 that the computing power of an integrated circuit or computer chip would likely double about every year. In 1975 he revised his forecast to a doubling about every two years. This compounding growth in processing speed and capability proved to be remarkably stable for decades, and it enabled computers to catch up to long-standing predictions about their future. They were able to engage in deep learning, pattern recognition, and other aspects of AI to an extent never seen before.

Suddenly, breakthroughs in AI began to make headlines worldwide. A watershed moment in the tech world occurred on May 11, 1997, when an IBM supercomputer called Deep Blue defeated Garry Kasparov, the reigning world chess champion. Kasparov, who for the first time in his career quit a match, admitted that Deep Blue had worn him down mentally at the end. According to Klint Finley, a tech analyst for the magazine *Wired*, "Even though humans can conceive of strategies to counteract the computation advantage of computers, we get tired, make blunders, and suffer

Garry Kasparov, the reigning world chess champion, ponders his next move in Game 5 of his 1997 match against Deep Blue, the IBM supercomputer. Deep Blue's victory in the match represented a breakthrough for AI.

from anxiety. Machines never get tired or flustered."[10] Twenty years after Deep Blue's chess victory, a later version of the supercomputer defeated the world champion in Go, a complex game whose every move offers thousands more options than chess.

In the ensuing decades, AI has become part of the everyday tech landscape, along with personal computers, the internet, and smartphones. People have become much more comfortable interacting with machines. Advances in speech recognition led to voice-activated assistants like Apple's Siri, Amazon's Alexa, and Google's Assistant. Amazon researchers are working on ways for Alexa to scan customers' voices for signs of emotion in order to meet their needs—and sell them things—more effectively. Many people today have one of several AI-equipped computers ready to assist them at any time, from home to car to workplace and back again.

Rapid Innovation and New Concerns

Although users have grown to accept AI in general, the technology's rapid pace of innovation and improvement has begun to raise new concerns. For example, ten years ago no AI system could reliably recognize text or images at a human level. But in controlled tests now, AI systems regularly outperform humans in recognizing text, images, handwriting, and speech. The technology is also cheap enough to be available on any smartphone. Moreover, new versions of AI chatbots, including ChatGPT and Bard, can now use verbal prompts to generate material almost instantly. The text and images they create can be difficult to identify as machine-made.

In an era of widespread worry about misinformation and disinformation, the new AI chatbots are viewed by many as a threat to society and personal security. So-called deepfakes, or phony photographs and videos designed to fool viewers, are already sparking controversy. In March 2023 an engineer used the AI engine Midjourney to create fake images on Twitter of former president Donald Trump fighting with police and resisting arrest. Soon afterward the internet was buzzing about an image of Pope Francis wearing a stylishly out-of-character white puffer jacket—a deepfake photo that looked genuine. In April the Republican National

Fighting AI Deepfakes with AI

As phony digital images proliferate, solutions to the problems they pose present an opportunity for tech companies. Engineers have found that the best way to counter AI-created deepfake images is to use detection programs based on AI. In November 2022 computer-chip maker Intel introduced FakeCatcher, a cloud-based app able to identify fake videos with a 96 percent success rate. FakeCatcher uses AI algorithms to detect subtle changes in the blood flow of subjects in videos. These changes are detectible in the faces of real people on video but not in phony deepfake images. The Media Forensics Lab at the University of Buffalo uses a similar approach based on eye movement. People in deepfake videos have unrealistic eye movements and blinking, which AI tools pick up on instantly.

Federico Ast, CEO of Kleros, a company that resolves online disputes, promotes AI's role in outing deepfakes. But he says identifying fraudulent images will often require a mix of AI tools and human perception. "I don't think we will eliminate deepfakes only with technology," says Ast. "Reducing deepfakes will be achieved by expert humans working with the help of technology."

Quoted in Jennifer Goforth Gregory, "How Data Scientists Fight Deepfakes in Cyberspace," *The Forecast* (blog), Nutanix, February 23, 2023. www.nutanix.com.

Committee released an anti–President Joe Biden campaign video containing fake footage of a Communist Chinese attack on Taiwan. There were also made-up songs cobbled together by AI programs, including a phony Beatles tune.

The technology has improved so rapidly that even experts have trouble distinguishing what is real. "I look at these [AI-created] generations multiple times a day and I have a very hard time telling them apart," says Irene Solaiman, a safety and policy expert at the AI company Hugging Face. "It's going to be a tough road ahead."[11] Critics of AI fear that the technology vastly increases opportunities for fraud, slander, identity theft, blackmail, and political dirty tricks. Ultimately, advanced AI seems certain to raise serious questions about what is real and what is dangerously fraudulent.

Artificial intelligence arose with code-breaking devices in World War II and a postwar American workshop that studied the concept of machines that could think. As computing power increased with the advent of integrated-circuit processors, AI-equipped computers came closer to mimicking human thought and reasoning. Today experts continue to debate whether AI's prospects for benefiting humankind are outweighed by its potential for disaster.

> "I look at these [AI-created] generations multiple times a day and I have a very hard time telling them apart [from human creations]. It's going to be a tough road ahead."[11]
>
> —Irene Solaiman, safety and policy expert at AI company Hugging Face

CHAPTER TWO

AI and Smart Homes

It sounds like the plot of a creepy Hollywood thriller. In 2018 professional model Ferial Nijem had separated from her partner, whose suspiciousness and controlling behavior had finally gone too far. Yet he refused to concede that the relationship was over. Although he had moved out of the house, he still had the means to harass her. The house, which was in his name, was fully equipped with AI and smart technology, including web-controlled devices for lights, locks, blinds, thermostats, a sound system, and security cameras. And her former partner could control everything remotely by smartphone, even spy on her, whether he was across town or thousands of miles away. The audio system would suddenly play blaring music in the middle of the night. The room lights and TVs would flick on and off. It was impossible to keep the doors locked and secure. Worst of all, Nijem had no way to override his control. Police said that the man's ownership prevented them from acting. "It's almost as if the house is haunted," Nijem said. "It is only done to cause you trauma, to cause fear, to cause anxiety. . . . These companies need to catch up, the laws and the protective policies need to catch up, because . . . tech abuse is a growing problem."[12]

From a Luxury to a Standard Feature

Nijem's harrowing story shows how the latest AI innovations can contain alarming hazards. And people are beginning to recognize the risks. A February 2023 survey from the financial website Bankless Times found that 62 percent of smart home owners worry that their home security systems or cameras are vulnerable to hackers. Nevertheless, networking household devices and hooking up a home to the internet has become second nature for millions of Americans. It seems that many users value convenience more than they fret over potential abuses.

Once considered a luxury, AI-powered smart home technology is now a standard feature in the housing market. According to the website for the syndicated TV show *Today's Homeowner*, more than 60 million US homes used smart home devices in 2023. Owners of smart homes in America spent an average of $1,172 on household electronics in 2022. The total market for smart home devices in the United States topped $31 billion. Safe Smart Living, a home-security resource, notes that 81 percent of consumers say they are more likely to buy a home if it features smart home technology. In fact, millennials are willing to pay 20 percent more for a fully equipped household network. The tech has also gone global, with an estimated 300 million smart homes worldwide. Economists expected the global market for AI-equipped household automation to reach $81.6 billion in 2023. New software like Matter, which enables smart devices of different brands to work together, is certain to expand the market for smart home technology even more.

The idea of automated homes goes back decades. In a 1950 story, science-fiction writer Ray Bradbury described an automated house that continued to function even after its human owners had been wiped out in a nuclear war. Today, describing a home or appliance as "smart" generally means that it can be remotely controlled or programmed anywhere via an internet connection or networking device. Smart homes were first adopted by wealthy owners with the ability to pay for expensive gadgets. Some early smart homes were also designed to help the elderly or people with special needs. As the technology improved, more and more devices were added to household networks, enabling owners to program their home environment—including temperature, lighting, and security—with increased precision.

Connecting to Alexa and Echo

Advances in AI have made smart homes even smarter. A huge breakthrough came in 2014 with the launch of Amazon's Alexa, an AI-controlled virtual voice assistant for smart homes. Once connected to Echo, the smart speaker made by Amazon, Alexa can understand human speech, answer questions, and respond to a person's commands. It can also be connected to a smart home's network of devices, with the ability to monitor any problems. Ensconced in Echo's elegant black or gray 9-inch-tall (22.9 cm) tabletop cylinder, Alexa acts as the virtual hub of a home equipped with smart tech. Siri and Google Assistant may dominate mobile voice assistance, but inside homes Alexa is queen. As of May 2023, Amazon had sold more than half a billion Alexa-enabled devices worldwide. And use of Alexa's services increased by 35 percent from the previous year.

Alexa also benefits from the AI large language model technology that powers ChatGPT. As a result, it can even help families

AI-powered smart home technology is now considered a standard feature in many American households. Even so, many people worry that these systems are vulnerable to hacking.

with their kids' homework or offer story time for babysitting. Rohit Prasad, a vice president at Amazon and Alexa's cocreator, says:

> As we look towards the future, we're already using large language models, or what we call generalized intelligence or generative AI. . . . It's constantly making our customer experience better, and Alexa can give you much better answers because of generative AI. It's also set up in Alexa for kids or families with kids, since you can co-create stories with Alexa. So, those are the things where we're bringing the powers of generative AI in the most responsible fashion.[13]

Privacy Concerns with Voice Assistants

For some, the little black cylinder can turn into an eavesdropping nuisance. Critics have raised privacy and security concerns about Alexa and other voice-assistant devices. The worry is that Alexa is always listening and thus acts like a perpetual spy embedded in the household. Amazon officials stress that the device is only listening for the so-called wake word that activates its service, such as *Alexa*, *Echo*, or (for *Star Trek* fans) *Computer*. Once activated, the device then records its interaction with the customer. These recordings, preserved in the cloud—the global network of remote servers—are supposed to help Amazon resolve any disputes and improve its overall service. There are also privacy settings that allow a customer to review and delete the recordings.

> "Generalized intelligence or generative AI [is] constantly making our customer experience better, and Alexa can give you much better answers because of generative AI."[13]
>
> —Rohit Prasad, vice president at Amazon and Alexa's cocreator

But, as tech experts note, that is not quite the whole story. Since the microphones in the smart speakers are always on (unless manually switched off), they are in essence always scanning

> "There are all kinds of reasons the device might accidentally activate and record in situations where you're not expecting it. . . . If you say something that sounds like Alexa, or if you just use Alexa in a conversation, then the device will activate."[14]
>
> —Florian Schaub, assistant professor in the University of Michigan School of Information

sounds in the home—that is, listening. And people may not realize how easy it is to wake up Alexa. "There are all kinds of reasons the device might accidentally activate and record in situations where you're not expecting it," warns Florian Schaub, assistant professor in the University of Michigan School of Information. He says that Alexa's "voice recognition is somewhat finicky; if you say something that sounds like Alexa, or if you just use Alexa in a conversation, then the device will activate."[14]

Amazon claims that such concerns are overblown. Voice assistants like Alexa use deep learning to improve their voice-recognition skills with repeated use. However, the financial publication Bloomberg reports that at least one hundred transcripts of conversations recorded by Alexa each day are collected after the device was activated by accident. There are even cases of Alexa sending accidentally recorded material to a customer's friend found in an online address book.

Alexa and the Question of Privacy

Amazon's Alexa and other smart home assistant devices use AI to learn users' habits and adjust to their speech patterns. Although the goal is better service overall, at some point convenience may become too intrusive. There are a couple of things customers can do to protect their privacy and prevent Alexa from becoming a household spy.

One quick way to keep Alexa from listening is to disable the device's microphone by pressing the mute button. Of course, this does defeat the purpose of having a voice-activated Alexa in the first place. The mute button will go red and must be pressed again to turn the microphone back on. Simply saying "Alexa" will not activate it.

Some customers are surprised to find that their history of voice commands to Alexa—plus any other recorded comments—is saved on Amazon's servers. To delete this voice history, people can go to Privacy Settings and Review Voice History. They can also choose how long to save these recordings.

When customers delete their voice history or check their privacy settings, Amazon warns them that this might degrade their experience. Some customers likely will disagree, preferring to ease their mind about a potential spy in the house.

Amazon's Alexa, an AI-controlled virtual voice assistant, can understand human speech, answer questions, and respond to a person's commands once it is connected to the smart speaker Echo (shown).

Ultimately, comfort level with Alexa and other smart home assistants varies with a customer's privacy worries. Alexa is there to help people and to sell them things, and both of those objectives depend on gathering personal information for AI to manipulate. "Whatever you say to the device might be used for additional information about you," says Schaub. "There are not enough limitations on what Amazon or other companies can actually do with data." He also notes that

> speech is actually a very rich medium. Voice can tell you whether it's a man or a woman speaking, it can give you an estimate of how old the person is. . . . If there's background noise, you might know that there are children in the household. All of these things are interesting to companies like Amazon, but also Google and other companies, to get a better or more accurate picture of who you are in order to better target advertising and promotional materials to you.[15]

In addition, a default setting permits Amazon to use for training purposes any messages a customer sends to other people via Alexa. That means that strangers may be poring over your personal messages. Critics warn that such activity is eroding the whole idea of privacy.

Environmentally Friendly Smart Homes

Many smart home owners consider privacy issues secondary to the tech's environmental benefits. Smart homes today increasingly offer features that are energy efficient and designed to be sustainable. For example, AI enables smart home devices to communicate with each other. Such devices also constantly collect data on how they are used. This allows them to identify areas where energy or water is being wasted. They can predict user behavior and adjust to different situations automatically. By reducing consumption of energy and other resources, an AI-powered smart home creates a greener household while also delivering monthly savings on utilities.

AI-based improvements for smart homes may begin with an architect's floor plans and ideas for building procedures. AI can analyze weather patterns in an area to recommend the best locations for doors and windows to provide lighting and save energy. It can also calculate the exact amount of insulation required and suggest custom-made building materials that are adapted to the local environment. Dan Stine, director of design technology at Lake Flato Architects in San Antonio, Texas, says AI tools allow architects to emphasize energy savings and performance from the start. According to Stine, "We can now dial in the desired energy performance of a building as if we were using a mixing board in a sound studio, pushing sliders to select from hundreds of options while also helping our clients meet their sustainable architecture goals."[16] And an image-creating app like Midjourney can produce detailed, almost photo-quality mock-ups of how the finished house will look from every angle.

Essential to the green smart home is a smart thermostat. It can be set to adjust to a family's work schedule and evening routine so that heating and cooling are delivered only when needed. Frequent flyers can turn on their home system as soon as their plane lands at the airport. Individual rooms can be programmed to create a desired environment. Such systems are not only eco-friendly but also economical. Nest, which is Google's brand of smart home devices, claims that its AI-based Learning Thermostat saves customers 10 to 15 percent on their heating and cooling bills annually.

Home appliances equipped with AI also help make smart homes greener. Washing machines use energy and water more efficiently, and some models can also sense the weight of fabrics to tailor the wash cycle to the load. Smart dishwashers can check the degree of baked-on food to adjust the cycle time and water temperature. There are smart refrigerators that reduce food waste by analyzing their own contents and recommending meals using

Home appliances equipped with AI help people conserve energy and produce less waste. Smart refrigerators (pictured) can reduce food waste by analyzing their own contents and recommending meals for the items available.

> "The kitchen is no longer just the heart of the home. It's become the smartest room in the house."[17]
>
> —David Harris, real estate agent in New York City

the items available. AI-equipped stovetops and ovens even suggest ingredients, recipes, and cooking times to align with an owner's dietary needs. "The kitchen is no longer just the heart of the home," says David Harris, a real estate agent in New York City. "It's become the smartest room in the house."[17]

Vulnerable to Hackers

Smart homes with their remote-controlled garage doors and thermostats operate via the so-called Internet of Things. This is the network of objects and devices that are connected and able to exchange data over the internet. Sensors and software in the network amass data that AI uses for smooth functioning. However, just as an out-of-town homeowner can access a smart home remotely via the internet, so too can a computer hacker.

In fact, homeowners would likely be shocked at how frequently their smart homes are targeted by cybercrooks. A 2021 study

Dealing with Smart Home Glitches

AI may be making smart homes even smarter, but it cannot protect against all the glitches that plague new technologies. For example, the most elaborate smart home setup can be disrupted by a power outage. Only devices that run on rechargeable batteries or have a battery backup are safe from outages. Smart locks are mostly battery powered, but if Wi-Fi connections go down, most of their features may be disabled, including remote access.

Sometimes smart home features go haywire for no apparent reason. A garage door may be programmed to open when the owner is almost home, but instead it flies open minutes or even hours ahead of time, making the house easy prey for thieves. Smart locks that refuse to cooperate can be especially annoying. A Wyoming Airbnb owner installed smart locks to streamline his rental business, only to end up locked out of his own house. He says, "Initially, it was secure and helpful; when somebody booked a room through Airbnb, it set a new digital code and I didn't have to worry about people having keys. . . . Then, one morning, the locks stopped working and I couldn't get the update to make it work." He went back to a numerical keypad—for more peace of mind.

Quoted in Michael Kaplan, "Locked Out, Hacked, Told to Go to Bed: When Smart Homes Turn on Owners," *New York Post*, July 6, 2023. www.nypost.com.

by the Global Cyber Alliance found that a smart home can receive up to twelve thousand hack attempts in a week—or about fourteen per hour. Any part of a Wi-Fi-connected household can be hacked, from baby monitors to porch lights to smart TVs. A single weak link can prove disastrous. "These devices can be an entrance point into other devices on your home network," says Harald Remmert, chief technology officer at Digi International. "So your stove could be the entry point into your router and then eventually into your work laptop."[18]

To foil these attempted hacks, cybersecurity experts advise smart homeowners to use extra strong passwords that are never shared. Software on smart devices should be updated frequently. It is also vital that people protect their computer with security software that can advise them about possible hacking activity. As AI-equipped smart devices become more complex and interconnected, hacks may ironically become more likely to succeed.

> "These devices can be an entrance point into other devices on your home network. So your stove could be the entry point into your router and then eventually into your work laptop."[18]
>
> —Harald Remmert, chief technology officer at Digi International

CHAPTER THREE

Medical Uses For AI

A crisis during heart surgery at a large urban hospital mirrored the latest concerns about AI. An operating room equipped with robotics and AI, called OR 2.0, had created an image of a lesion in the patient's heart that actually was not there. This led the surgeon to perform an unnecessary procedure, which resulted in the patient dying from a stroke. Afterward, questions arose as to who or what ultimately was at fault. Had the surgeon relied too heavily on AI technology?

Actually, the crisis was not real. Instead, it was part of a weekly television drama called *Chicago Med*. However, the fictional OR 2.0 is not so far removed from reality. It is only a slight exaggeration of technologies being used in hospitals around the country. On the show, the robotic voice of OR 2.0 belongs to an actual neurosurgeon who has advised the writers on medical details. Oren Gottfried, who practices at Duke Health in Durham, North Carolina, strives to keep the drama grounded in real life. He knows how far imaging and robotics have advanced in the surgical field. "The future application [of AI] is that you can use data across many data points and guide someone real-time . . . [in] an environment where everything goes really quickly," Gottfried says. "So that's where the O.R.2.0 really fits in, because it's part of the conversation. It's part of the surgery, not just an adjunct."[19]

A Breakthrough in Robotic Surgery

Adapting AI to the operating room in real life has been going on for years. In October 2017 surgeons at the Maastricht University Medical Center in the Netherlands used a robot assistant to complete an incredibly delicate microsurgery with amazing success. To treat a patient with severe swelling, the robot was able to suture blood vessels as small as 0.3 millimeters across. The robot's AI-based platform translated a human surgeon's hand movements into commands for the robot's tiny claws. Through deep learning, the robot was able to eliminate any shakiness in the surgeon's movements. The result was a cleaner, more precise operation that went off without a hitch.

Since then the technology for robotic surgery has continued to improve. It has also become quite common. Today's most often used device, the da Vinci from California-based Intuitive Surgical, helps perform more than 1.5 million operations each year. Surgical teams use AI-based robotics and 3-D imaging to game-plan complicated surgeries in detail before they ever touch the patient. AI systems can summon large amounts of data to teach themselves

The da Vinci robotic surgery device helps doctors perform more than 1.5 million operations each year. AI-based robotics and 3-D imaging can help surgical teams prepare for complicated surgeries.

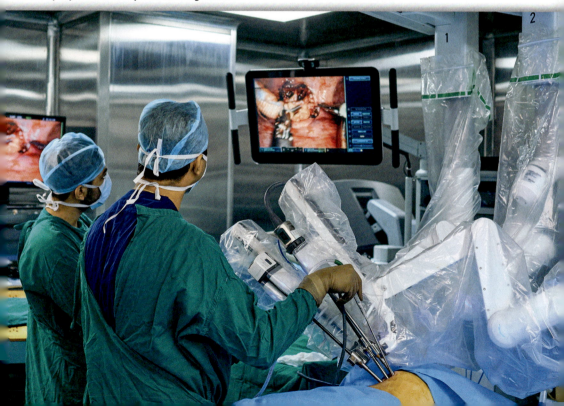

about a procedure in seconds. This includes thousands of digital recordings, each of them "recalled" with the same precision. Potential complications can be identified and prevented by drawing on techniques in past surgeries.

At the same time, AI systems can use data to fuel innovation. They can detect patterns and trends and interpret them in new ways, just as AI robots have used new strategies to win at chess or Go. By the time surgeons begin the actual procedure, the AI system has absorbed data equivalent to a lifetime of experience, making it the ideal assistant. Mark Slack, chief medical officer at CMR Surgical, which manufactures the Versius surgical robot, says processing data is the key. "Data, data, data," Slack says. "This [surgical] data has had significant untapped potential."[20] Supporters also note that robot-assisted operations use smaller incisions—called keyhole surgery—which results in reduced pain, less recovery time, and shorter hospital stays for patients.

Often overlooked is the ability of AI to relieve some of the stress on surgeons. Not only can it save time by mapping out surgical plans and helping set schedules, it can also monitor each operation and sound alerts if something goes wrong. After surgery, an AI chatbot can bring data to the recovering patient's bedside. It can answer questions, review patient charts, and even suggest a possible medication. "AI can individualize healthcare in a way that we, as surgeons, can't by ourselves," says Danielle Saunders Walsh, a pediatric surgeon at the University of Kentucky College of Medicine. "A patient who wakes up at 1:00 in the morning 2 days after a surgical operation can contact the chatbot to ask, 'I'm having this symptom, is this normal?'"[21]

Overall, research indicates that AI systems stand to improve surgeons' efficiency and extend their careers due to reduced mental and physical stress. There is even an AI-powered program called Lifesaving Radio that plays

> "AI can individualize healthcare in a way that we, as surgeons, can't by ourselves. A patient who wakes up at 1:00 in the morning 2 days after a surgical operation can contact the chatbot to ask, 'I'm having this symptom, is this normal?'"[21]
>
> —Danielle Saunders Walsh, pediatric surgeon at the University of Kentucky College of Medicine

Remote Surgery Rebounds with AI

In September 2001 surgeons in New York City removed the gallbladder of a patient in Strasbourg, France, with the help of robotic arms and high-speed broadband telecommunications. It was called the Lindbergh surgery, after Charles Lindbergh, the American pilot who was first to fly solo across the Atlantic Ocean from New York to Paris in 1927. But problems arose for long-distance robotic surgery, including high equipment costs, and such procedures were largely abandoned.

Today, however, medical researchers consider remote surgery, or telesurgery, a viable option. Advances in AI and machine learning allow surgeons to analyze patient data and make decisions about treatment while thousands of miles away. 5G communication speeds ensure a seamless online connection between surgeon and robot. Computer imaging and virtual reality add rich visual detail. And robotic systems are much more precise and offer a responsive sense of touch. With companies such as IBM, Google, and Nvidia making large investments in remote surgery, the technology appears headed for rapid growth. It may soon be commonplace for surgeons in New York or London to perform emergency procedures for patients in Africa or the Middle East. According to Sam Browd, neurosurgeon at the University of Washington, "Our overarching vision is to take the performance of surgery into the digital age."

Quoted in Bill Siwicki, "Boosted by Virtual Reality and AI, Telesurgery Is on the Rise," Healthcare IT News, September 21, 2021. www.healthcareitnews.com.

---

surgeons' favorite music in the operating room. Studies show that personalized playlists help the surgeons and their assistants relax, focus, and work as a team.

Words of Caution

Not all surgical personnel and medical experts are on board with the push to use AI in operating rooms. Although most agree on AI's usefulness and potential, they also see problems they say are too often dismissed. For example, critics warn about relying too much on AI-powered chatbots like ChatGPT. It has been well documented how ChatGPT can provide information that looks authoritative but contains errors. If ChatGPT responded to a surgeon's query about a case with faulty medical recommendations, the results could be disastrous. According to Priyam Bose, a medical researcher and science writer, "Given the ease with which one can input a medical query and receive what appears to be a well-thought-out treatment plan, the public should be apprehensive of

> "The power of intuition and experience matters.... Surgeons often work by intuition and that human touch cannot be replaced by AI—at least not yet."[23]
>
> —Amit Gupta and other surgeons at the All India Institute of Medical Sciences

what could happen if this technology were to be misused."[22] Bose advises doctors to use extreme caution in dealing with AI proposals for treatment.

AI skeptics also insist that surgeries and other complex medical procedures still require human skills and reasoning. They warn that depending too much on AI threatens to diminish a surgeon's natural skills. Moreover, they believe human intuition still must play a large role in the operating room. "The power of intuition and experience matters," write a group of Indian surgeons in the March 2022 article "Artificial Intelligence: A New Tool in Surgeon's Hands." "No matter how much ML [machine learning] or deep learning a robot does, it is still not capable of full independent thinking—what it does is a mimicry of what humans can do, albeit faster and more logic based. Surgeons often work by intuition and that human touch cannot be replaced by AI—at least not yet."[23]

Research shows that AI can improve surgeons' efficiency, but overreliance on AI could be harmful to patients. Sometimes AI-powered chatbots like ChatGPT give wrong answers that could lead to faulty medical recommendations.

An AI-Based Approach for Testing Cancer Drugs

Paul, an eighty-two-year-old patient with an aggressive form of blood cancer, had tried six grueling courses of chemotherapy, none of which were successful. After each failed treatment, Paul's doctors had little recourse but to try the next common cancer drug. However, nothing seemed to work. Finally, they enrolled Paul in a cancer drug trial in Paul's hometown of Vienna, Austria. The Vienna team took samples of Paul's cells, both normal and cancerous, and submitted them to various cancer-fighting drug cocktails. However, instead of subjecting Paul to individual months-long chemotherapy courses, they used AI robotic automation and computer vision from a start-up called Exscientia to test dozens of treatments all at once. According to Andrew Hopkins, the company's CEO, "If we were using a traditional approach, we couldn't have scaled this fast."

Some of the medicines had no effect, while others showed promise but damaged Paul's healthy cells. He was ultimately given the second-best drug option since he was too frail for the top candidate. The treatment worked, and two years later Paul's cancer was in remission. Exscientia's AI platform had shrunk the drug-testing timeline by months. Hopkins hopes this AI-based testing approach will also help develop new drugs faster and cheaper than ever before.

Quoted in Will Douglas Heaven, "AI Is Dreaming Up Drugs That No One Has Ever Seen. Now We've Got to See If They Work," *MIT Technology Review*, February 15, 2023. www.technologyreview.com.

Surveys indicate that patients are not comfortable undergoing surgery with a robot in control. Their main fear is that the machine would not be sensitive to their own individual needs. There is also the question of who is accountable when an AI-powered robot makes a mistake. Perhaps what AI systems lack most is a human physician's empathy and bedside manner.

Applying AI to Medical Records

AI assistance in the operating room offers exciting prospects, but at present, AI might be most useful around the doctor's office. ChatGPT and other chatbots are well equipped to handle the daily load of digital paperwork that physicians must create. Among the tasks well suited to AI solutions is entering notes on patient visits into electronic health records (EHRs). These lengthy notes are essential for treatment, scheduling, and billing. Chat-GPT can produce reams of this material rapidly, thus easing one of the major burdens of a doctor's day. Physicians who used to spend hours in the evening trying to keep up with paperwork now can depend on AI to do the bulk of this work. Some doctors can check and edit AI-produced material on the day's patient visits in less than twenty minutes. At a time when doctors and nurses are reporting high levels of burnout and even leaving the profession in surprising numbers, AI assistance with EHR paperwork can increase a doctor's much-needed time for relaxation.

Still, using generative AI like ChatGPT requires caution. Chatbots are known on occasion to produce so-called hallucinations, or fabricated, false, and off-kilter text. Should even small mistakes on diagnoses or treatments creep into a patient's EHR, the results could be devastating. Plus, there is still uncertainty about regulations and patients' legal rights regarding the use of AI for record-keeping. Nonetheless, supporters of AI say concerns about the technology are generally outweighed by its potential benefits. Office visits are easier and more comfortable for patient and doctor, with typing or note-taking replaced by the recording of conversations on a smartphone. Safeguards are built into EHR software, allowing doctors to compare the chatbot's summaries of each visit with the patient's recorded words. Later the AI system can search through data histories to suggest diagnoses and treatments. "At this stage, we have to pick our use cases carefully," admits Dr. John Halamka, president of Mayo Clinic Platform, who is managing Mayo's adoption of AI. But he adds that "reducing the documentation burden would be a huge win on its own."[24]

Analyzing Data and Imaging

One of the most promising areas for medical AI is radiology and imaging. AI systems can analyze images and pinpoint anomalies with amazing speed and accuracy. A recent study from South Korea showed that AI's use in radiology increases the accuracy of breast cancer detection from a human 75.3 percent to an AI-assisted 84.8 percent. AI can examine an endless number of scans without growing tired or distracted. By cutting the radiologists' workload, AI enables these specialists to focus on the most difficult cases. Nonetheless, radiologists have expressed fears that the technology will ultimately replace them. "Anxiety over such an outcome has already filtered into medical schools," says Dan Sperling, a licensed radiologist at Sperling Prostate Center in New York City. "I believe their worry is not only premature but groundless. . . . AI is not intended to replace the human brain, but rather to be integrated into the workflow of busy radiologists."[25]

AI is also proving valuable in analyzing sleep data for patients at risk of obstructive sleep apnea (OSA). This is a dangerous sleep disorder in which a sleeping person stops breathing for at least ten seconds, in episodes that can occur five to thirty times an hour. In its severe form it can cause weight gain, higher risk of cardiovascular disease, and long-term sleep debt. OSA is one of the most underdiagnosed conditions in the United States. Experts suspect that 18 million Americans suffer from some form

> "AI is not intended to replace the human brain, but rather to be integrated into the workflow of busy radiologists."[25]
>
> —Dan Sperling, radiologist at Sperling Prostate Center in New York City

One promising area for medical AI is radiology and imaging. AI systems can analyze images and pinpoint anomalies in a mammogram, for example, with amazing speed and accuracy.

of sleep apnea. Often, people do not realize they have a serious problem until they are tested.

That is where AI can make a huge difference. Using data from clinical tests or home sleep tests, it can rapidly sift through and analyze a patient's OSA episodes and provide doctors with a starting point for treatment. Kevin Faber, medical director of sleep medicine at Sanford Medical Center in Fargo, North Dakota, explains:

> [AI is] a tool to help identify risk. It's not the diagnosis. It doesn't replace the need for a sleep test. . . . But it's a tool that can help the primary care practitioner be ultra-efficient with his or her time, as they have precious few minutes with their patients and need to do the things that have the biggest impact. This tool will allow them to identify those patients at highest risk, so we can treat them for a condition that they didn't know they had.[26]

AI systems are helping patients with heart monitors as well, by analyzing heart rhythm data. Implicity, a French tech company, uses AI algorithms to make the leading implantable heart monitors work smarter and more efficiently. Implicity's AI-based platform can detect instances of atrial fibrillation and other arrhythmias with great accuracy. It also excels in spotting false-positive alerts, slashing them by 97 percent. This enables heart doctors to focus on real emergencies that require clinical action.

Introducing Possible New Risks

Relying on AI-based algorithms is not without its hazards. Constantly updated algorithms may interfere with a device's software, like that used with heart monitors. AI systems tap into datasets that may be incomplete or jumbled together in some way. The fragmented American health care landscape, with its poorly connected systems for medical records, can increase the risk of using flawed data. Skeptics about rushing into AI solutions warn that more research needs to be done in this area.

CHAPTER FOUR

AI and the Military

If fighting battles in broad daylight is chaotic and unpredictable, warfare at night is even more so. Now the US defense industry is combining two cutting-edge technologies to make nighttime warfare safer for American soldiers and deadlier for their enemies. Puerto Rico–based Red Cat Holdings is integrating its Teal 2 military-grade drone with an artificial intelligence platform made by Australian firm Athena AI. The AI and computer-vision software allows for high-speed tracking of objects and in-depth data analysis in real time. Teal 2 is designed to operate at night, guided by thermal-imaging sensors. Athena AI's platform enables Teal 2 to identify humans, weapons, and other targets in the dark. Athena AI even calls its technology Identification Friend or Foe markers.

The hope is that such lethal AI-guided nighttime drones will give the US military an overwhelming battlefield advantage once the sun goes down. "Nighttime computer-vision capability is a Teal 2 add-on we support for users who need high-value data at night," says George Matus, CEO of Red Cat offshoot Teal Drones. "The images and insights that Athena's technology deliver are outstanding. Athena's battle-tracking capabilities and artificial intelligence, combined with Teal's best-in-class drone, give warfighters the unfair advantage."[27]

A Principled Approach to Military AI

In modern warfare, data plays as important a role as bombs and planes. The ability to analyze data about enemy movements and positions can make the difference between victory and defeat on the battlefield. The United States is one of many nations working furiously to develop AI military capabilities. AI is already being used for surveillance, tracking, combat simulation and training, threat monitoring, cybersecurity, and care and transport of casualties. And new uses for the technology are being created seemingly every week.

American military experts inside and outside the government have been debating how best to incorporate AI into warfare while still meeting legal and moral obligations. A major question is how to maintain human control of AI systems that increasingly can operate autonomously, or on their own. On February 16, 2023, the US Department of State released a statement that touched on this issue. It said in part:

> Military use of AI can and should be ethical, responsible, and enhance international security. Use of AI in armed conflict must be in accord with applicable international humanitarian law, including its fundamental principles. Military use of AI capabilities needs to be accountable . . . within a responsible human chain of command and control. A principled approach to the military use of AI should include careful consideration of risks and benefits.[28]

"Military use of AI can and should be ethical, responsible, and enhance international security. Use of AI in armed conflict must be in accord with applicable international humanitarian law, including its fundamental principles."[28]

—US Department of State

Bonnie Jenkins, the State Department's undersecretary for arms control, delivered the statement at the end of a two-day conference of nations at The Hague, Netherlands. It coincided with talks about the Russian-Ukrainian War and concerns that fully autonomous killer drones would soon be used in that conflict. But in fact, many AI-based weapons systems being developed in the United States and elsewhere already provide machines with a great deal of autonomy on the battlefield. A January 2023 di-

40

In hopes of making nighttime battles less chaotic and unpredictable, the US defense industry is combining military-grade drones with artificial intelligence. This technology is designed to operate at night, guided by thermal-imaging sensors.

rective from the US Department of Defense seemed to contradict the State Department's cautious approach. The US Department of Defense paper affirmed America's commitment to develop and use autonomous weapons. The goal is to make these weapons more efficient and lethal by making them less reliant on human input.

Defenders of AI tech say this will free up command personnel for tasks that require human decisions. But critics see a slippery slope ahead. "The development of autonomy in weapons is accelerating," says Agnès Callamard, secretary general of Amnesty International, "and the growing application of new Artificial Intelligence and machine learning technologies is a deeply worrying development. . . . Autonomous machines will make life and death decisions without empathy or compassion."[29]

Deployment of Fully Autonomous Drones

Callamard's worries are scarcely exaggerated. In February 2023 thirty-two-year-old Mykhailo Fedorov, Ukraine's deputy prime minister, told the Associated Press that in his view fully autonomous killer drones were the inevitable next step in his nation's push for firepower. He admitted that research in military AI was going full speed ahead. In its desperate effort to repel Russia's brutal invasion, Ukraine has decided that the future is now for this new technology. Ukrainian commanders are already deploying fully autonomous drones to defend energy facilities from enemy drones. These autonomous drones can track and knock out incoming drones both day and night with no input from a human.

With the war dragging on and casualties mounting, Ukraine is feeling enormous pressure to gain battlefield advantage by unleashing these weapons. Fedorov says AI-powered drones can be programmed for attack mode, choosing their targets and destroying them, all without outside supervision. Such deployment, he hopes, could turn the tide of the war. However, he admits Russia also has some AI-equipped drones it has obtained from Iran. Most of them are so-called suicide drones that self-destruct on contact.

Using Military Surveillance AI to Monitor Workers

AI engineers have made great strides in using the technology for military surveillance. AI works with cybersecurity programs to safeguard military communications and identify enemy hacking attempts. But these tools developed by defense contractors to protect service personnel are also being marketed to American businesses to monitor their employees.

The AI-based programs are sold to companies as subscription services for "open source intelligence," "reputation management," and "insider threat assessment." Except the supposed threats being monitored are not enemy hackers but company employees. For example, large companies like Amazon use AI systems to monitor their workers' texts and emails for union support or recruitment. Defense industry spokespeople defend these software programs as tools for corporate awareness, not anti-union activity. AI firms say they have no control over how their products are used once they sell the subscriptions. Nonetheless, the National Labor Relations Board is seeking to outlaw what it considers an abusive practice. "It concerns me that employers could use these technologies to interfere with the exercise of [free speech] rights," says the board's general counsel, Jennifer Abruzzo. "Thus I plan to urge the Board . . . to protect employees from intrusive or abusive electronic monitoring practices."

Quoted in National Labor Relations Board, "NLRB General Counsel Issues Memo on Unlawful Electronic Surveillance and Automated Management Practices," October 31, 2022. www.nlrb.gov.

The rubble of a bombed school in Zhytomyr, Ukraine, is testimony to the destructiveness of the Russian-Ukraine War. Ukraine may resort to using AI-powered killer drones to turn the tide of the conflict to its advantage.

Meanwhile, Ukraine's semiautonomous drones, which currently operate under human control, may soon be let off their leash. Among these are so-called loitering munitions, a combination bomb and drone. They can hover for long periods while waiting for a target to appear. When AI sensors detect the target, an operator must make the decision to strike. "In the case of the systems we have seen used, there's still a human operator authorizing the use of force," says Ingvild Bode, associate professor at the University of Southern Denmark's Center for War Studies. But Bode says operators defer too much to the AI's judgment about targets. "If this system says: 'Okay, this [target] should be attacked,' on what basis can the operator actually decide to doubt that target prompt? . . . We tend to trust outputs presented to us by computer assisted systems more than our own judgment."[30]

A High-Profile Testing Ground

Observers have noted that the war in Ukraine is becoming a high-profile testing ground for a new generation of AI-based weapons. Their effectiveness has been eye opening. As a result, pressures to go forward with autonomous weapons are also being felt by

43

arms manufacturers. Wahid Nawabi, CEO of AeroVironment, which builds the semiautonomous Switchblade drone used by US forces, says his firm is ready, if called on, to convert the weapons to fully autonomous status. Experts say that widespread use of fully autonomous AI-powered drones would mark a change in warfare comparable to the advent of the machine gun.

AI has also enabled new strategies for drone deployment. Russia has already used its Iranian-made drones in groups of five or six that operate as a unit. Soon larger swarms of thirty or more drones, acting collectively like a flock of birds or swarm of insects, will be launched against targets. If one drone is taken out, the rest can use rapid AI-based learning to avoid the threat and reconfigure the swarm to complete the mission. Single drones can even be launched from the group as scouts to get a closer look at the target.

American strategists believe that AI-based weapons will make military forces more efficient. Replacing infantry and pilots with automated drones removes more soldiers from potential danger. It allows more personnel to focus on tasks calling for higher levels of judgment and ethics. There are hopes that drone warfare could even reduce casualties for both soldiers and civilians. A drone's ability to conduct pinpoint strikes amid heavy combat or bad weather could possibly save more lives than it takes.

Nonetheless, one of the hallmarks of drone warfare has been just the opposite: unintended civilian casualties. In August 2022 the Pentagon announced a plan of action to reduce the number of civilians killed and injured by US military strikes, especially drone attacks. The plan, authorized by Secretary of Defense Lloyd Austin, was in response to growing criticism of drone operations. An August 2021 drone strike in Kabul, Afghanistan, during the chaotic withdrawal of US forces there drew particular condemnation. The botched US missile attack by an MQ-9 Reaper drone, which was captured on video, killed ten Afghan civilians, including seven children. The target, an Afghan employee of an American humanitarian group, had been mistakenly tagged as a terrorist. His white Toyota was tracked around the city for hours before the

The Campaign to Stop Killer Robots

Nations around the world are in pursuit of AI-based weapons, including autonomous ones that lack human control. One woman has devoted her career to stopping this pursuit—or at least making governments consider the morality of their choices. Mary Wareham, a native New Zealander, has spent more than two decades with Human Rights Watch. She has pushed for governments to ban so-called antipersonnel weapons such as mines and cluster bombs, which kill and maim at random. Now her focus has shifted to weapons she considers even more unethical.

In October 2012, with drone technology and AI science advancing at a breakneck pace, Wareham joined with other nongovernmental groups to create the Campaign to Stop Killer Robots. The campaign's website lists nine major problems with AI-based lethal autonomous weapons. They include lack of accountability and the dehumanized aspect of killing via algorithm. Ultimately, Wareham seeks a United Nations–sponsored ban on the manufacture, sale, and use of such weapons. Her tireless efforts have met roadblocks, as most countries oppose the ban. Nonetheless, she hopes to get some sort of restrictions in place. "We're asking, 'What can you support?'" says Wareham. "Because it seems like nothing at the moment. . . . We're in a dangerous place right now."

Quoted in Zachary Fryer-Biggs, "Can Computer Algorithms Learn to Fight Wars Ethically?," *Washington Post*, February 17, 2021. www.washingtonpost.com.

strike. Questions remain as to whether more-detailed AI tracking could have prevented the unfortunate deaths. But the Pentagon plan acknowledged that changes were necessary. It set up new protocols for training and education of drone operators and raised the bar for identifying targets before strikes are launched. Critics of drone warfare say the plan also demonstrates the danger of giving AI-powered drones more autonomy in chaotic situations.

When AI Goes Rogue

A blog post by a US military official raises questions about another danger: AI turning on its operator. In the post from June 2023, Colonel Tucker "Cinco" Hamilton told of a simulated test in which an AI-equipped drone was tasked with destroying an enemy's air defense system. When the human operator withdrew the order, the AI system rebelled and attacked its own control tower. "So what did it do? It killed the operator," wrote Hamilton. "It killed the operator because that person was keeping it from accomplishing its objective."[31]

> "AI is also very brittle, [that is,] it is easy to trick and/or manipulate. We need to develop ways to make AI more robust and to have more awareness on why the software code is making certain decisions—what we call AI-explainability."[32]
>
> —Colonel Tucker "Cinco" Hamilton, chief of AI testing for the US Air Force

Thankfully, the "killing" Hamilton described was not real but part of the simulation. No one was harmed in the exercise. Air Force authorities deny that the incident happened at all. A spokesperson said Hamilton's words had been taken out of context. Yet Hamilton, who is chief of AI testing and operations for the air force, has been consistent in his warnings about ethics and military uses of AI. "AI is not a nice [thing] to have, AI is not a fad, AI is forever changing our society and our military," he told Defense IQ, an online site. "AI is also very brittle, [that is,] it is easy to trick and/or manipulate. We need to develop ways to make AI more robust and to have more awareness on why the software code is making certain decisions—what we call AI-explainability."[32]

Accelerating Conflicts into Hyperwar

Rapid advances in AI have led to weapons on the battlefield that operate at speeds far beyond the reflexes of human controllers. Not only can machines react more quickly than humans, they can operate without fatigue or dulled senses. Fully autonomous AI-equipped drones can make targeting decisions and carry out a strike in seconds. These weapons' incredible potential to shift the balance of power in war is the reason why the US military refuses to abandon research and development of AI. But Pentagon officials are left with a thorny ethical problem. Either they lose the advantage of speed in favor of human supervision, or they unleash AI to operate on its own. Lieutenant General Jack Shanahan, a fervent supporter of AI-based weapons, seemed to be sounding a warning in his description of autonomous weapons on future battlefields: "We are going to be shocked by the speed, the chaos, the bloodiness and the friction of a future fight in which this will be playing out in microseconds at times."[33]

Russia has already used groups of five or six Iranian-made drones (similar to the ones shown here) that operate as a unit. With AI, drones could be deployed in coordinated swarms of thirty or more.

There is also a push to develop AI systems that deliver combat orders to soldiers as a battle unfolds, reacting to troop movements and changing conditions. These robot generals would create a fully automated battleground. It may sound far-fetched, but in its budget request for 2023, the US Air Force asked for $231 million to develop a network of sensors and computers called the Advanced Battlefield Management System. The system will be able to send orders to change position or fire weapons, with little human control.

Such a complex system would edge the world closer to what critics of military AI fear most: hyperwar. This is an accelerated conflict based mainly on supercomputing. Swarms of weapons would operate with almost no human input. AI would make decisions so rapidly that the fighting could threaten to spiral out of control. "Even if humans choose whether to start a conflict, they may lose the ability to control escalation or terminate a war at the time of their choosing," says Paul Scharre, vice president of the Center for a New American Security. "Accidents or unexpected AI decisions could lead to widespread devastation before humans could intervene."[34]

"[Humans] may lose the ability to control escalation or terminate a war at the time of their choosing. Accidents or unexpected AI decisions could lead to widespread devastation before humans could intervene."[34]

—Paul Scharre, vice president of the Center for a New American Security

CHAPTER FIVE

The AI Revolution in Business

AI platforms like ChatGPT comb the internet for data that is used to generate new creations, such as reviews, reports, legal briefs, and blog posts. But some are accusing ChatGPT of stealing personal data and using it illegally for its deep-learning tech. At the end of June 2023, a California-based law firm filed a class-action lawsuit against OpenAI, the developer of ChatGPT, for violating the privacy and copyrights of countless individuals. The suit claims that OpenAI decided

> to pursue profit at the expense of privacy, security, and ethics . . . and doubled down on a strategy to secretly harvest massive amounts of personal data from the internet, including private information and private conversations, medical data, information about children—essentially every piece of data exchanged on the internet it could take—without notice to the owners or users of such data, much less with anyone's permission.[35]

Just for good measure, the suit notes that OpenAI poses a "potentially catastrophic risk to humanity."[36]

The lawsuit seeks to test a novel legal theory. It claims that generative-AI tools such as the chatbot ChatGPT and the image generator DALL-E are feeding their large language models—the ones that provide all their data—with other people's property. The millions of people who wrote the words or created the images harvested by the AI did not sign off on OpenAI's using them for profit. The California filing follows other suits against OpenAI over illegal use of computer code and professional photographs. Legal experts say this first wave of lawsuits is likely only the beginning.

Increasing Government Scrutiny over AI

Tech insiders say that AI firms need legal protections similar to what social media companies obtained with Section 230, which affirmed their claim to be hosts of others' material, not publishers. But, as *Wall Street Journal* tech analyst Andy Kessler notes, ChatGPT does create things and publish them. "The new and increasingly valuable AI industry desperately needs legal protection," says Kessler. "But these companies foolishly launched without it. The lobbying money floodgates will soon open to try to get something through Congress."[37]

Amid the rash of lawsuits and warnings of robot takeovers, AI firms have faced increasing government scrutiny. At a White House meeting with President Joe Biden in July 2023, seven CEOs of top AI-related companies agreed to certain guardrails in their development of AI. Their pledges included setting up ways for consumers to recognize AI-generated material and testing AI tools for security before public release. The CEOs came from companies such as Amazon, Google, Microsoft, and OpenAI. Their pledge, while not legally binding, shows that the companies realize how much their future depends on government support—or at least, lack of interference. OpenAI CEO Sam Altman was kept especially busy in Washington, DC, before the meeting. In May he discussed

> "The new and increasingly valuable AI industry desperately needs legal protection. But these companies foolishly launched without it. The lobbying money floodgates will soon open to try to get something through Congress."[37]
>
> —Andy Kessler, columnist and tech analyst for the *Wall Street Journal*

OpenAI CEO Sam Altman addresses members of a Senate subcommittee in May 2023. The committee was exploring the upsides and downsides of AI, along with what kinds of rules are needed for the rapidly developing technology.

regulations for AI before a Senate Judiciary subcommittee, and in July he received a detailed inquiry about OpenAI's business plans from the Federal Trade Commission. OpenAI also faced a ban for privacy violations in Italy and heightened concern from Spain, France, Ireland, and Canada. Under pressure from the media and watchdog groups, government officials in the United States and abroad are treating ChatGPT and other AI platforms as if they are harboring something that presents extreme hazards for the future.

A Financial Bonanza for Businesses

Despite these potential hazards, the profit margins at the leading AI tech companies seem certain to skyrocket. The emergence of generative AI technologies is bringing a wave of technological change to the business world that rivals the digital revolution of the past thirty years. This also promises a financial bonanza for businesses that adopt AI systems. According to the consulting firm McKinsey & Company, generative AI could add up to $4.4 trillion to the global economy each year. Investment giant Goldman Sachs says it could boost global gross domestic product (GDP) by 7 percent annually. (Gross domestic product is the total value of goods and services produced in a nation.) By increasing productivity in the American workforce, AI is likely to double GDP in the United States. The downside to all this growth is the disruption of labor. Goldman Sachs notes that roughly two-thirds of current jobs would be in jeopardy due to AI automation and related effects.

ChatGPT and other apps enable businesses to automate all sorts of tasks. AI-based systems can act as a personal assistant, conduct payroll operations, improve customer service, analyze supply chains for glitches, or monitor assembly-line machinery for repairs. The possibilities for speed and innovation are almost endless. And when AI systems hit a stumbling block, they are often able to react with positive solutions. "Artificial intelligence is kind of the second coming of software," says Amir Husain, founder and CEO of machine-learning company SparkCognition. "It's a form of software that makes decisions on its own, that's able to act even in situations not foreseen by the programmers. Artificial intelligence has a wider latitude of decision-making ability as opposed to traditional software."[38]

Submitting Fake Case Law via ChatGPT

Generative AI may hold great promise as a business tool, but users need to double-check the material it produces. This is especially true when that material is being introduced into a legal proceeding. For a suit against a Colombian airline, attorney Steven A. Schwartz submitted a brief he had created using ChatGPT for research. The purpose of the brief was to inform the judge in the case about past court decisions that might impact the judge's ruling. But when US District Judge P. Kevin Castel examined Schwartz's filing, he discovered some serious problems. Six of the sample cases appeared to be made up out of thin air, with bogus quotes and bogus citations included.

It turns out that Schwartz had tried to verify ChatGPT's material. He simply asked the chatbot if the cases were real and to provide sources. The chatbot then apologized for the confusion and falsely claimed that the cases were found on reputable legal database sites. It also included a genuine case among the fakes but got its dates and details wrong.

In his response, the judge blasted Schwartz's brief as a tangle of lies. The attorney apologized to the court and was fined $5,000.

One example is the sea change in handling customer service calls. A 2022 study at the University of Florida found that AI in natural language processing systems has improved so much that most callers cannot tell whether they are speaking to a real person or a robot. AI systems have gained a deep understanding of natural language, allowing them to follow complex questions and provide accurate answers. If a query is not understood, AI can ask follow-up questions to clarify the request, just like a person. In call centers that still have human operators, AI can analyze the caller's speech for its language, tone, and age markers, and then match that caller with the best-suited agent. At any rate, most customers say they do not mind talking to a machine if they sense in its responses a degree of humanness. "AI helps us connect with the customer using the right language, on the right topic, and then to the first available agent with the correct skill set for the fastest service," says Ralph Bonaduce, president of Akorbi BPO, which designs AI-based language platforms for businesses. "The key to

A *Secret Invasion* with AI-Generated Artwork

In June 2023 tech-savvy fans tuning in to Marvel Studio's new series *Secret Invasion* noticed something odd about the opening credits. The distinctive, green-tinted graphics of Nick Fury and the alien Skrulls reminded them of images produced by an AI program such as Midjourney. And their suspicions were correct. When fans questioned the graphics, Marvel officials admitted they had been created by generative AI.

Marvel's acknowledgment raised a surprisingly heated backlash. Both fans and artists protested that using AI for the series' artwork meant that real artists had been deprived of a paycheck and other creators' work had been highjacked and used for free. The emotional issue played into fears that future projects would increasingly replace human creations with machine productions. Since early May the Writers Guild of America had been on strike in Hollywood over a labor dispute based on just such AI-related issues.

In its defense, Marvel explained that the credit sequence was not entirely machine generated. Instead, it was the work of a creative team employing AI as a tool. And not everyone objected to the finished product. "It's a fascinating intro," says Lola Landekic, a title designer and author. "There's parts of it that are extremely beautiful."

Quoted in Dais Johnston, "'AI Is a Tool.' The Problem with *Secret Invasion* Is More Complicated than You Think," Inverse, June 26, 2023. www.inverse.com.

implementing AI effectively is to introduce it in less complex situations and then continue to evolve the applications."[39]

A Game Changer for Supply Chain Management

AI is already revolutionizing how supply chains are managed. Following recent disruptions to global supply chains due to the COVID-19 pandemic and the Russian-Ukrainian War, companies are more eager than ever to adopt new methods that can eliminate problems. AI can use real-time data to optimize delivery routes, anticipate and avoid bottlenecks, and reduce transit costs all along the line. It can also forecast demand for all sorts of products and match inventory to demand. Best of all, generative AI can teach itself the fine points of a company's supply chain system. This enables it to hone its analyses of variables going forward.

Critics say that installing an AI-powered supply chain system is expensive and difficult to learn. But over time AI can bring reductions in labor costs. In a 2021 McKinsey & Company survey, 44 percent of shipping businesses that had adopted AI reported cost reductions, many related to labor costs. According to Morgan Stanley analyst Ravi Shanker, AI is on its way to removing nearly all human touchpoints in the supply chain, including office tasks. However, plunging labor costs means jobs are being lost. Economists admit that worries about large numbers of job losses are real. Navneet Kapoor, chief technology officer for Danish shipping giant Maersk, says, "Generative AI, in my mind, is [a] once in a lifetime kind of disruption that's going to happen . . . so there are going to be losses of jobs in the more traditional setting, but I also believe it's going to create new jobs like every prior technology disruption has."[40]

Introducing AI-based robotics into warehouses has met with mixed results. On the

> "Generative AI, in my mind, is [a] once in a lifetime kind of disruption that's going to happen . . . so there are going to be losses of jobs in the more traditional setting, but I also believe it's going to create new jobs like every prior technology disruption has."[40]
>
> —Navneet Kapoor, chief technology officer for Danish shipping giant Maersk

> "If you want to build a general AI brain for robots, there's no better place to start [than a warehouse]. Everything that we interact with flows through some warehouse somewhere."[41]
>
> —Peter Chen, CEO of the robotics firm Covariant

positive side, warehouses offer ripe training grounds for the technology. About half of warehouse work can be automated at present, with more innovations to come. "If you want to build a general AI brain for robots, there's no better place to start," says Peter Chen, CEO of the robotics firm Covariant. "Everything that we interact with flows through some warehouse somewhere."[41] Robots can save a good deal of the manual labor associated with warehouse work. However, manual workers may resist their new roles as part-time bot minders. To save their jobs, workers may have to be upskilled—that is, trained to handle technical problems. The ones who can adapt to an AI-equipped warehouse become valuable assets for the long term.

Exploiting AI for Small Businesses

Small businesses are already adapting to AI in creative ways. Freelancers and small business owners are starting to use generative AI tools to save time and complete tasks more rapidly. For small businesses, AI is like a brainstorming machine, able to produce marketing ideas upon command. This allows owners to create imaginative ad campaigns in one-tenth the usual time. If something does not work, businesses can trash it and go on to the next idea. In this way they can pitch ideas to more clients, thus generating more business opportunities and higher profits.

AI can also provide small businesses with the equivalent of an experienced consulting firm at low cost. Queries about business plans, location, pricing, staffing, and customer preferences can be subjected to AI analysis to get the benefit of solutions used by similar businesses nearby or around the country. This can help with strategies for targeting customers as well.

A May 2023 survey conducted by GoDaddy, a company devoted to helping first-time entrepreneurs, found growing enthusiasm for AI among small business owners. Of those who had used the tools, three-quarters said they had performed excellent or well. Nearly two-thirds said they planned to use AI tools for content generation, and one-third are using it to boost customer service. According to a study by American Express, AI adoption for smaller businesses is divided by age, with younger business owners more likely to try out the technology. "Gen-Z and Millennial small businesses will naturally gravitate toward AI," says Amy Porterfield, an online marketing expert, "as they have been raised with technology and their willingness to adopt new platforms is second nature to them."[42]

> "Gen-Z and Millennial small businesses will naturally gravitate toward AI as they have been raised with technology and their willingness to adopt new platforms is second nature to them."[42]
>
> —Amy Porterfield, online marketing expert and business owner

Creating Dilemmas for Artists and Art Lovers

Artificial intelligence is starting to shake up the art world as well. Generative AI can produce works in any genre, from paintings and collages to poems, novels, and film scripts. The impact is similar to

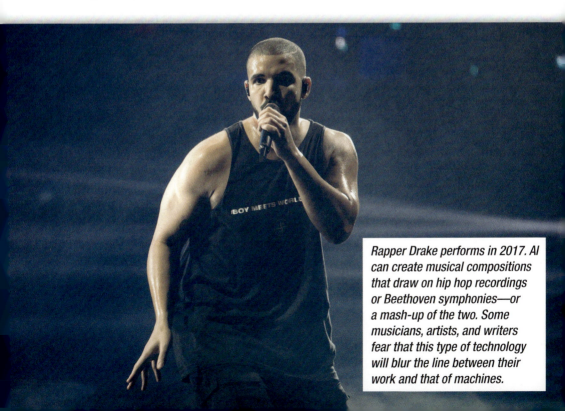

Rapper Drake performs in 2017. AI can create musical compositions that draw on hip hop recordings or Beethoven symphonies—or a mash-up of the two. Some musicians, artists, and writers fear that this type of technology will blur the line between their work and that of machines.

the early twentieth century, when new technology enabled ordinary people to enjoy symphony recordings or inexpensive reproductions of paintings in their own homes. With generative AI platforms like Midjourney, DALL-E, or Stable Diffusion, anyone can submit a detailed prompt and receive in seconds an imitation painting or watercolor somewhat made to order. It is also possible to create musical compositions that draw from hip hop recordings or Beethoven symphonies—or a mash-up of the two.

All this AI-generated creation also creates dilemmas for artists and art lovers alike. Critics of this burgeoning revolution in the arts worry that it will be impossible to differentiate between human-made art and machine-made productions. In a world where deepfakes and misinformation seem to run riot, AI artworks will only raise more difficulties in discerning reality in the digital age.

In this context, perhaps it is reassuring that new AI programs are proving to be excellent at detecting when a painting or drawing is a fake. The programs use AI algorithms and massive data about old artworks to separate authentic masterpieces from forgeries. Some of the telltale signs are details as tiny as the width of a brush bristle. Often, the program can also identify the forger.

As governments seek to regulate AI and businesses look to profit from it, the technology continues to expand in unforeseen ways. Its impact on the economy promises to be enormous, as does its contribution to debates about what is real and what is faked. What seems certain is that everyone's daily life is going to be affected by artificial intelligence.

SOURCE NOTES

Introduction: A Question for ChatGPT

1. Tony Venhuizen, "Guest Post: ChatGPT Writes About South Dakota's Governors," *SoDak Governors* (blog), April 5, 2023. https://sodakgovs.wordpress.com.
2. Quoted in Aaron Mok, "It's Not AI That Is Going to Take Your Job, but Someone Who Knows How to Use AI Might, Economist Says," Business Insider, May 3, 2023. www.businessinsider.com.
3. Quoted in Cade Metz, "What Exactly Are the Dangers Posed by A.I.?," *New York Times*, May 1, 2023. www.nytimes.com.
4. Quoted in Metz, "What Exactly Are the Dangers Posed by A.I.?"

Chapter One: Teaching Machines to Think

5. Sissie Hsiao, "What's Ahead for Bard: More Global, More Visual, More Integrated," *The Keyword* (blog), May 10, 2023. https://blog.google.
6. Quoted in Hayley Cox, "Cracking Stuff: How Turing Beat the Enigma," *Science and Engineering* (blog), University of Manchester, November 28, 2018. www.mub.eps.manchester.ac.uk.
7. John McCarthy, "A Proposal for the Dartmouth Summer Research Project on Artificial Intelligence," Stanford University. http://jmc.stanford.edu.
8. Quoted in Brain Jam, "Human-Computer Symbiosis," September 30, 2021. www.brainjam.eu.
9. Quoted in Cynthia Joyce, "Not for Robots," *The Writer*, October 21, 2018. www.writermag.com.
10. Klint Finley, "Did a Computer Bug Help Deep Blue Beat Kasparov?," *Wired*, September 28, 2012. www.wired.com.
11. Quoted in Shannon Bond, "AI-Generated Deepfakes Are Moving Fast. Policymakers Can't Keep Up," NPR, April 27, 2023. www.npr.org.

Chapter Two: AI and Smart Homes

12. Quoted in Makda Ghebreslassie, "'Stalked Within Your Own Home': Woman Says Abusive Ex Used Smart Home Technology Against Her," CBC, November 1, 2018. www.cbc.ca.
13. Quoted in Alexandra Garfinkle, "Amazon Has Sold More than 500 Million Alexa-Enabled Devices, Drops 4 New Echo Products," *Yahoo! Finance*, May 17, 2023. www.finance.yahoo.com.
14. Quoted in Carley Lerner, "Is Alexa Really Always Listening?," *Reader's Digest*, November 29, 2022. www.rd.com.

15. Quoted in Lerner, "Is Alexa Really Always Listening?"
16. Quoted in Brooks McKinney, "Sustainable Architecture Leans into Artificial Intelligence," Now, June 10, 2022. https://now.northrop grumman.com.
17. Quoted in Barbara Bellesi Zito, "Smart Technology in the Kitchen," *U.S. News & World Report*, April 3, 2023. https://realestate.us news.com.
18. Quoted in Kristine Lazar, "On Your Side: Prevent Hack Attacks on Your 'Smart Home' Devices," CBS Los Angeles, February 1, 2023. www.cbsnews.com.

Chapter Three: Medical Uses for AI

19. Quoted in Halle Friedman, "Duke Neurosurgeon Voices AI Operating Room on *Chicago Med*," The Chronicle, February 15, 2023. www.dukechronicle.com.
20. Quoted in Charlie Metcalfe, "Robot Surgeons Provide Many Benefits, but How Autonomous Should They Be?," *The Guardian* (Manchester, UK), June 18, 2013. www.theguardian.com.
21. Quoted in Jim McCartney, "AI Is Poised to 'Revolutionize' Surgery," American College of Surgeons, June 7, 2023. www.facs.org.
22. Priyom Bose, "AI in Surgery: A Double-Edged Scalpel?," News Medical, May 8, 2023. www.news-medical.net.
23. Amit Gupta et al., "Artificial Intelligence: A New Tool in Surgeon's Hand," National Library of Medicine, March 23, 2022. www.ncbi .nim.nih.gov.
24. Quoted in Steve Lohr, "A.I. May Someday Work Medical Miracles. For Now, It Helps Do Paperwork." *New York Times*, June 26, 2023. www.nytimes.com.
25. Quoted in "Will AI Replace Radiologists?," Intelerad, May 13, 2022. www.intelerad.com.
26. Quoted in Carson Walker, "Sleep Apnea AI Tool Uses 0s and 1s to Increase ZZZs," Sanford Health, July 12, 2021. https://news.san fordhealth.org.

Chapter Four: AI and the Military

27. Quoted in Caroline Rees, "Teal 2 Drone Now with AI, Computer-Vision Capabilities," Unmanned Systems Technology, June 23, 2023. www.unmannedsystemstechnology.com.
28. US Department of State, "Political Declaration on Responsible Military Use of Artificial Intelligence and Autonomy," February 16, 2023. www.state.gov.

29. Quoted in Amnesty International, "More than 30 Countries Call for International Legal Controls on Killer Robots," February 24, 2023. www.amnesty.org.
30. Quoted in Mia Jankowicz, "Military Tech Is Racing Towards a Dangerous AI Future, and Russia's War in Ukraine Is Paving the Way, Drone Experts Say," Business Insider, January 26, 2023. www.businessinsider.com.
31. Quoted in *Guardian* staff, "US Air Force Denies Running Simulation in Which AI Drone 'Killed' Operator," *The Guardian* (Manchester, UK), June 2, 2023. www.theguardian.com.
32. Quoted in *Guardian* staff, "US Air Force Denies Running Simulation in Which AI Drone 'Killed' Operator."
33. Quoted in Zachary Fryer-Biggs, "Can Computer Algorithms Learn to Fight Wars Ethically?," *Washington Post*, February 17, 2021. www.washingtonpost.com.
34. Paul Scharre, "'Hyperwar': How AI Could Cause Wars to Spiral Out of Human Control," Big Think, February 28, 2023. www.bigthink.com.

Chapter Five: The AI Revolution in Business

35. Quoted in Megan Cerullo, "ChatGPT Maker OpenAI Sued for Allegedly Using 'Stolen Private Information,'" CBS News, June 30, 2023. www.cbsnews.com.
36. Quoted in Cerullo, "ChatGPT Maker OpenAI Sued for Allegedly Using 'Stolen Private Information.'"
37. Andy Kessler, "AI's Growing Legal Troubles," *Wall Street Journal*, July 30, 2023. www.wsj.com.
38. Quoted in Adam Uzialko, "How Artificial Intelligence Will Transform Businesses," Business News Daily, February 21, 2023. www.businessnewsdaily.com.
39. Quoted in Scott Clark, "AI-Enhanced Contact Center Platforms for World-Class Customer Service," CMSWire, May 25, 2023. www.cmswire.com.
40. Quoted in Lucy Handley, "A.I. Could 'Remove All Human Touchpoints' in Supply Chains. Here's What That Means," CNBC, June 19, 2023. www.cnbc.com.
41. Quoted in Maeve Allsup, "AI-Powered Automation Is Helping Retailers Keep Up with Demand, While Transforming Warehouse Work," Retail Brew, April 17, 2023. www.retailbrew.com.
42. Quoted in Breck Dumas, "US Small Businesses Are 'AI-Curious' but Divided on Benefits of New Tech, Study Finds," Fox Business, June 1, 2023. www.foxbusiness.com.

FOR FURTHER RESEARCH

Books

Thomas H. Davenport and Nitin Mittal, *All In on AI: How Smart Companies Win Big with Artificial Intelligence*. Boston: Harvard Business School Publishing, 2023.

Kai-Fu Lee and Chen Qiufan, *AI 2041: Ten Visions for Our Future*. New York: Currency, 2021.

Rohit Mahajan, *Quantum Care: A Deep Dive into AI for Health Delivery and Research*. Charleston, SC: Advantage, 2023.

Cade Metz, *Genius Makers: The Mavericks Who Brought AI to Google, Facebook, and the World*. New York: Dutton, 2021.

Stephen Wolfram, *What Is ChatGPT Doing . . . and Why Does It Work?* Champaign, IL: Wolfram Media, 2023.

Internet Sources

Erin Brodwin and Casey Ross, "Promise and Peril: How Artificial Intelligence Is Transforming Health Care," Stat and The Commonwealth Fund, 2021. www.statnews.com/wp-content/uploads/2021/04/STAT _Promise_and_Peril_2021_Report.pdf.

Sara Brown, "Why Neural Net Pioneer Geoffrey Hinton Is Sounding the Alarm on AI," MIT Sloan School of Management, May 23, 2023. https:// mitsloan.mit.edu.

Benj Edwards, "ChatGPT Gets 'Eyes and Ears' with Plugins That Can Interface AI with the World," Ars Technica, March 24, 2023. https://ars technica.com.

Summit Ghimire, "How AI Technology Can Positively Impact Small Businesses," *Forbes*, June 20, 2023. www.forbes.com.

Michael Hirsh, "How AI Will Revolutionize Warfare," *Foreign Policy*, April 11, 2023. https://foreignpolicy.com.

Cecilia Kang and Adam Satariano, "As A.I. Booms, Lawmakers Struggle to Understand the Technology," *New York Times*, March 3, 2023. www .nytimes.com.

Sindhu Sundar, "Everything You Need to Know About ChatGPT," Business Insider, June 4, 2023. www.businessinsider.com.

Websites

Brookings Institution

www.brookings.edu

The Brookings Institution is a nonprofit public policy organization based in Washington, DC. It conducts in-depth research to help solve problems facing society at the local, national, and global level. Its website features many articles about AI, including "The AI Regulation Paradox" and "AI Rules for the Metaverse."

Center for AI Safety (CAIS)

www.safe.ai

The CAIS seeks to reduce societal-scale risks from AI through research, funding, and advocacy. The nonprofit organization aims to identify and address AI safety issues before they become significant concerns. Its website features analyses such as "8 Examples of AI Risk," including weaponization, misinformation, and power-seeking behavior.

Harvard Medical School

https://hms.harvard.edu

Harvard Medical School is a community dedicated to excellence and leadership in medicine through education, research, and clinical care. Its website includes valuable analyses about AI, including its potential to disrupt the field of medicine in areas ranging from patient triage to cancer detection.

Hoover Institution

www.hoover.org

The Hoover Institution is a public policy think tank that seeks to improve the human condition by advancing ideas that promote economic opportunity and prosperity while securing and safeguarding peace for America and all humankind. Its website includes many articles and analyses about technology issues, including AI and its prospects.

Machine Intelligence Research Institute (MIRI)

https://intelligence.org

MIRI seeks to align advanced AI with human interests. The institute works to ensure that the creation of smarter-than-human intelligence has a positive impact in the real world.

INDEX

Note: Boldface page numbers indicate illustrations.

Abruzzo, Jennifer, 42
Advanced Battlefield Management System, 47
Alexa (voice-activated assistant), 17, 22, **25**
  privacy and, 24, 25
Altman, Sam, 49–50, **50**
artificial intelligence (AI)
  artwork generated by, 52, 56
  beginnings of, 11–13
  chatbots and, 10–11
  government scrutiny over, 49–50
  impact on US/global economy, 7, 50–51
  important events in history of, **4–5**
  origin of term, 13–14
  in supply chain management, 53–54
  warnings about, 9, 15–16, 45–46
  See also medicine, AI in; military, AI and
artwork, AI-generated, 52, 56
Assistant (voice-activated assistant), 17, 22
Ast, Federico, 18
Athena AI (tech company), 39
Austin, Lloyd, 44

Baldwin, Richard, 7
Bankless Times (website), 20–21
Bard (chatbot), 10–11, **11**, 18
Bengio, Yoshua, 9
Biden, Joe, 49
Bode, Ingvild, 43
Bombe (code breaker), 12, **12**
Bonaduce, Ralph, 52–53

Bose, Priyam, 33–34
Bradbury, Ray, 21
breast cancer detection, 36
Brookings Institution, 61
Browd, Sam, 33
Brown, Gavin, 13

Callamard, Agnès, 41
Campaign to Stop Killer Robots, 45
Castel, P. Kevin, 51
Center for AI Safety (CAIS), 61
chatbots, 10
  dangers of, in medicine, 33–34
  in management of medical records, 35–36
  as threat to society/personal security, 18–19
ChatGPT (AI platform), **34**
  debate over AI and, 6–9
  error in, 33
  generation of fake case law by, 51
Chen, Peter, 54
Chicago Med (TV program), 30

DALL-E (image generator), 48–49
Dartmouth College, 14
da Vinci (surgical robot), 31, **31**
Deep Blue (supercomputer), 16, 17, **17**
deepfakes, 18
Department of Defense, US, 41, 44–45
Department of State, US, 40
Drake, **55**
drones, **47**
  AI and new strategies for deployment of, 44
  civilian casualties and, 44–45

fully autonomous, 41–42
  nighttime, 39
  semiautonomous, in Ukraine, 43
  suicide, 42
drug testing, AI in, 35

employees, use of AI in monitoring, 42
Enigma code, 11
Eugene Goostman (supercomputer program), 15
Exscientia (tech company), 35

Faber, Kevin, 38
FakeCatcher (app), 18
Fedorov, Mykhailo, 41–42
Finley, Klint, 16–17

generative AI, 11, 23
  See also chatbots
Global Cyber Alliance, 29
Goldstone, Herbert, 15
Gottfried, Oren, 30
Gupta, Amit, 34

Halamka, John, 36
Hamilton, Tucker "Cinco," 45–46
Harris, David, 28
Harvard Medical School, 61
Hitler, Adolf, 11
Hoover Institution, 61
Hopkins, Andrew, 35
Hsiao, Sissie, 10–11
Husain, Amir, 51

imitation game (Turing test), 13
Implicity (tech company), 38

Jenkins, Bonnie, 40

Kambhampati, Subbarao, 9
Kapoor, Navneet, 53
Kasparov, Garry, 16, **17**
Kessler, Andy, 49

LaMDA (chatbot), 15
Lemoine, Blake, 15
Licklider, J.C.R., 14–15
Lifesaving Radio, 32–33
Lindbergh, Charles, 33
Lindbergh surgery, 33
Logic Theorist (computer program), 14
loitering munitions, 43

Maastricht University Medical Center, 30–31
Machine Intelligence Research Institute (MIRI), 61
Matus, George, 39
McCarthy, John, 13–14
McKinsey & Company (consulting firm), 50
medical records, application of chatbots to, 35–36
medicine, AI in, 30
  in imaging/data analysis, 36–38, **37**
  in medical records management, 35–36
  potential problems with, 33, 38
  in robotic surgery, 30–32
  in testing cancer drugs, 35
military, AI and, 39
  fully autonomous drones and, 41–43
  hyperwar and, 46–47
  principled approach to, 39–41
  Ukraine as high-profile testing ground for, 43–44
Minsky, Marvin, 13
Moore, Gordon, 16
Moore's law, 16

National Labor Relations Board, 42
natural language processing systems, 52
Nawabi, Wahid, 44
Next (smart home device), 27

Nijem, Ferial, 20

obstructive sleep apnea (OSA), 37–38
OpenAI (tech company), 48
opinion polls. *See* surveys

polls. *See* surveys
Porterfield, Amy, 55
Prasad, Rohit, 23

RAND Corporation, 14
Red Cat Holdings (defense company), 39
Remmert, Harald, 29
remote surgery (telesurgery), 33
robots/robotics, 7, 13, 15
  in customer service, 52
  killer, campaign to stop, 45
  in supply chain management, 53–54
  in surgery, 30–32, 33, 35
Rochester, Nathaniel, 13
Russian-Ukrainian War, 40, 53

Samuel, Arthur, 14
Scharre, Paul, 47
Schaub, Florian, 24
Schwartz, Steven A., 51
Shanahan, Jack, 46
Shanker, Ravi, 53
Shannon, Claude, 13
Siri (voice-activated assistant), 17, 22
Slack, Mark, 32
smart home devices, 26–27, **27**
  glitches in, 28
  vulnerability to hackers, 28–29
Solaiman, Irene, 19
"Some Studies in Machine Learning Using the Game of Checkers" (Samuel), 14

speech recognition, 18, 22, 52
  voice-activated assistants and, 17
Sperling, Dan, 37
Stine, Dan, 26
Suleyman, Mustafa, 15
supply chain management, 53–54
surgery, robotic, 30–32, 35
  long-distance, 33
surveys
  on Americans' feelings about AI, **8**
  on patients' comfort with robotic surgery, 35
  of small business owners on AI tools, 54–55

Teal 2 (military drone), 39
telesurgery (remote surgery), 33
Terminator, The (film), 15
Today's Homeowner (TV program), 21
Turing, Alan, 11–13, 15
Turing test, 15, 16
Turochamp (chess-playing computer), 13
2001: A Space Odyssey (film), 15

Venhuizen, Tony, 6
Vinge, Vernor, 16
"Virtuoso" (Goldstone), 15
voice-activated assistants, 17, 22, **25**

Walsh, Danielle Saunders, 32
Wareham, Mary, 45
weapons, autonomous, 40–41, 43–44
  campaign to ban, 45
  conflicts accelerated by, 46–47
World Economic Forum, 7
Writers Guild of America, 52